FIRST-TIME HOMEBUYER HERO

INSIDER TIPS & TRICKS FROM A REALTOR TO YOU

ZENA T.P. WILLIAMS

A Third Culture Kid Production

Copyright © 2024 by Zena T.P. Williams

All rights reserved. No part of this book may be reproduced, distributed, or transmitted in any form or by any means, including photocopying, recording, or other electronic or mechanical methods, without the prior written permission of the publisher, except in the case of brief quotations embodied in critical reviews and certain other noncommercial uses permitted by copyright law.

A Third Culture Kid Production - Self-Published by Author

Contents

APPRECIATION III

INTRODUCTION IX

CHAPTER 1: WHAT THEY WISH THEY KNEW 1

CHAPTER 2 AGENCY & THE NAR SETTLEMENT 9

CHAPTER 3: A LITTLE STORY ABOUT THE ART OF HOMEBUYING - DID RIGHTS AND COULD HAVE DONE BETTERS 27

CHAPTER 4: HOW TO EAT THIS ELEPHANT - HOME SHOPPING 41

CHAPTER 5: HOW TO EAT THIS ELEPHANT - THE PURCHASING PROCESS 47

CHAPTER 6: BE A SAVVY - BUYER SUGGESTIONS FOR WHAT TO LOOK FOR IN A COMMUNITY 61

CONCLUSION 65

APPRECIATION

A Journey Unlike Any Other: These acknowledgments were the most exhilarating part of putting this book together. You will not find literature like this elsewhere because the world of real estate is not yet set up for integration. It revolves around disparate but intricate processes, legal frameworks, and the wealth of insights from individual real estate agents who shape this dynamic market. What sets this book apart is that the stories within are real, lived experiences from genuine buyers and agents.

The Homeownership Advantage: Why purchase a home? With the surge in home prices, an interesting phenomenon takes place – homeowners swiftly ascend the ladder of wealth compared to their renting counterparts. The act of owning real estate does not just secure a roof over your head; it substantially augments your net worth. This, in turn, unlocks a wealth of life and income opportunities, solidifying a path toward financial stability and prosperity.

Numbers That Startle: Back in 2014, the National Association of Realtors (NAR) made a revelation – 87% of real estate agents do not make it past their first five (5) years in the business. Think about that for a moment. The resilient 13% that remain are not just survivors; they have become genuine experts in the field. These are the individuals and teams who uplift fellow agents, guide clients, and pass on vital knowledge that nurtures the industry's strength and energy. So, when you find a great realtor, support them by letting your circle know you value them. This industry thrives on recommendations, and it is a tough business.

Mom: The Beacon of Support: The first nod of gratitude goes to my mother. When I returned from my life abroad in 2015, a tabula rasa awaited me. She stepped up and offered to cover the expenses of my real estate license and initial education, providing a lifeline as I navigated new beginnings. Little did I know that a simple license would swing open the doors to some of the most profound opportunities. Fast forward to 2023, and I am on the brink of graduating from Georgetown University with a master's degree in real estate on top of my license to practice that I have held since 2016. Remember, real estate is not just a career; it is a game-changer. I owe a big thanks to my mother, who, as a realtor herself, offered her support in my practice. She also approached me about writing a book and here we are.

An Aunt's Steady Presence: A heartfelt acknowledgment goes to my aunt in Philadelphia, Marolyn Bailey. She has been that steady hand keeping me balanced on the precipice of uncertainty all these years. While I am often the go-to person for clarity, it's worth noting that even those who provide guidance need shoulders to lean on. To my aunt, your support is immeasurable, and it is wrapped in boundless love. It is like the Sir Isaac Newton quote that says, "If I have seen further it is by standing on the shoulders of Giants". Much gratitude goes to what I call the solutions architecture of the Westview Associates Inc.

Liz Coleman: The Guiding Star: Continuing the acknowledgment parade, enter Liz Coleman—a local luminary who stepped into her own spotlight in 2023 by launching Liz Coleman Realty, her very own brokerage firm. A seasoned realtor with a treasure trove of experience, she has fast-tracked my path and enriched my understanding of residential real estate intricacies. Liz's generous sharing of wisdom is destined to have a ripple effect, already enhancing the real estate landscape in Houston, TX.

Contributors with Heart: The individuals who grace these pages with their experiences and insights have truly added their unique perspectives to this book. Many of them are not just fellow practitioners or business partners outside of real estate; they are property owners who willingly joined me in my inaugural literary journey. What sets them apart? It is their willingness to peel back the layers, and openly provide feedback and even stories in the upcoming section called "What They Wish They Knew" and beyond. Bianca Kowal, Jordan Foy (Jordan Foy Fashion Files), John Bramblett, Jose Nieto, Rayven J. Moore (Houston Drip Factory), Tamia Amano (her alias), Terri King (CRE Broker, Atlanta), Mike Phung, Tash (her alias).

Surrounded by Excellence: Among these contributors, I have consciously surrounded myself with people who are ceaselessly driven toward their life aspirations. Looking back at the voyage of writing this book, I'm humbled by the robust support network that bolstered me. Their sage counsel and unwavering encouragement are not just empty words; they've sparked actions and empowered my journey.

A Grateful Acknowledgment to Myself: Finally, a special note of appreciation to none other than myself. While I share my thoughts through blogging on my personal site, zenatpwilliams.com, embarking on the journey of writing and designing a book is an entirely new and exhilarating adventure for this Third Culture Kid. It is an adventure that hasn't been easy. Still, I embrace it and am committed to seeing it through.

Venturing into Uncharted Territory: Why? Because this material is a dire necessity, an unmet need that begs for attention. I also believe in my capacity to deliver a product of unwavering quality. Homebuyers deserve more than just trickles of advice in passing; they need a profoundly specialized reference. This endeavor is my contribution to an industry I hold close to, alongside my continuous growth. Contribution to society is an integral source of personal fulfillment, and I can confidently say that it's a feeling like no other.

INTRODUCTION

Welcome to the essential guide for first-time homebuyers! Whether you're taking your first steps or looking for a refresher after purchasing a home in the past, this book is your ultimate companion. Say hello to added clarity and value-added commentary.

Inside these pages, you'll find not just stories but a breakdown of the core principles of homebuying without going into too much detail in areas outside of my expertise. If you want to learn more about a subject outside of residential real estate, please review sources with related expertise. My goal is to equip you with the knowledge you need right at the point of sale and throughout the process. It is understandable that the process can be overwhelming, especially if you're a first-time buyer. However, fear less! This guide is designed to empower you with insights that will not only clarify your journey but also ease some of your worries.

Please also take into consideration that each real estate transaction is unique, involving various parties, from realtors to lending and title teams. That's why this literature delves into the specifics, ensuring you understand who plays what role. You'll gain a crystal-clear understanding of responsibilities, expectations, and the steps to maintain a smooth path toward a successful homebuying experience.

It's important to remember that no two deals are alike, but armed with the information provided, you'll be well-prepared to navigate the complexities. By the time you finish, you'll be ready to embark on your homebuying journey with confidence and excitement. Get ready to make informed decisions and embrace the adventure of finding your dream home!

By: Zena T.P. Williams

Chapter 1:

WHAT THEY WISH THEY KNEW

Owning a home isn't just a financial investment; it's an emotional one too. With the right approach, purchasing a home can become one of life's most fulfilling experiences. So, take that leap forward – I promise, it will change your life! Here's a roadmap based on my own journey, packed with lessons myself and others learned and valuable tips to help you unravel the intricacies of being a first-time homebuyer.

Through sharing this information, I hope to broaden your perspective. So, listen to or read this as many times as it takes as I know it is a lot of information. While you might not anticipate every twist and turn, there are strategies to position yourself for overall success. By the way, if you're on the brink of your home purchase, a big CONGRATULATIONS is in order! My aim as a licensed realtor is to impart wisdom as you embark on this exciting journey.

Let's kick things off with reflections on the hindsight of individuals in my circle. They've revealed the things they wish they had known before diving into their first home purchase.

Bianca, ~35 years old, Sr. Investment Officer (owner, single-family home residence)

This is strictly for cold climates, but Bianca and her family wish they had known the different heat sources. It would also have been nice to better understand the condition of older items like their roof. A roof is a major item, and the seller should provide information in a Seller's Disclosure (SD) about the age and condition upon request.

Ultimately, the condition is evaluated by your inspector who will be able to tell you what you are getting into.

When they purchased the home in 2019, they hadn't considered the layout of the house for long-term use. After having two kids, they are finding the stairs to be tedious. Their home choice could have also had a more open floor plan. They primarily bought for location. I personally think that living near one of the most beautiful beaches in Maine is somehow worth the stair struggle. However, I am not there daily. If I were, I would probably have bought into an open floor plan as well. Note to self.

Jordan, ~32 years old, Tax Consultant (owner, single-family home residence)

Jordan's experience resonates with raw honesty. She wishes she had been more aware of the financial implications tied to owning an older home. Her story revolves around a captivating flip constructed back in 1940. The initial purchase granted her an automatic equity boost of approximately $50,000.00, an appealing prospect. Yet, beneath the charming exterior lay concealed foundation and plumbing issues, a costly revelation. How costly? The first year of homeownership demanded an unexpected $30,000.00 of out-of-pocket expenses, unearthing the reality that aesthetics often do not reveal the complete story. An ostensibly thorough inspector missed crucial red flags, leaving Jordan blindsided by underlying issues. Jordan's journey involves more than just financial surprises. Amidst the contract work and renovations, contractors often directed their inquiries and decision-making questions toward her husband although she is a member of the LGBT community and solely owns the property. This dynamic adds another layer of complexity, necessitating her heightened vigilance about her safety and sense of security. Jordan's narrative may strike a chord with many, echoing the sentiment that home ownership is not always the picturesque dream it is often portrayed to be. For individuals like me, a solo homeowner, her story resonates. It serves as a reminder that homeownership for women, particularly those without a male presence, comes with a distinct set of considerations and challenges, transforming the notion of security into a comprehensive protocol. Despite the investment of time, money, and effort, true enjoyment of her home has been somewhat elusive. Her experience shines a light on the importance of informed decision-making, thorough inspections, and a nuanced understanding of the unique challenges that homeowners face.

Jose, ~28 years old, Residential Real Estate Agent (owner, single-family home residence)

Jose is a sharp residential real estate agent in the Houston, TX area. When he bought his first home circa 2021, he expressed that he wished he had known about currently available programs that offer terms like 100% financing for eligible candidates and no requirement of private mortgage insurance (PMI).

Rayven, ~30 years old, CPA, Oil & Gas (owner, multi-family property)

Rayven boldly decided to purchase a multi-family home during the uncertainty of the COVID-19 pandemic. Rayven offers some helpful advice: approach inspectors' findings with caution. While they may identify some of a home's issues, approximately 25%, he contends that the remaining problems will likely manifest within the first three years of home ownership.

Rayven's perspective explores the intriguing idea that previous homeowners may not always prioritize thorough repairs. Instead, they may focus on superficial solutions that ensure a smooth sale. This is also evident in Jordan's story, where hidden problems were concealed. While this is not always the case, it is a common theme that resonates with many homebuyers. In hindsight, Rayven identifies a key aspect he wishes he had been better prepared for, the substantial effort required to maintain a large property, especially if one is unaware of its true history. His experience centers on owning an expansive multi-family home that occupies nearly half a city block near the University of Houston. As he acknowledges, this ambitious undertaking demonstrates the immense challenge of overseeing and maintaining a large property for a first-time homeowner.

Tamia, ~36 years old, Commercial Real Estate Professional (owner, multi-family property)

Tamia works in corporate real estate for a top global firm. She was a residential agent before purchasing her home. The item she wishes she had known about was the final closing costs. In the reading, you will hear about the estimate of cost and the closing disclosures (CDs). Unfortunately, the estimated closing costs presented up front are rarely the same as the final closing costs. So, get your reserves ready.

> **Terri, ~37 years old, Principal Broker, Commercial Real Estate Firm (owner, single-family home residence)**

Terri's advice is to put everything on a maintenance schedule. Going in, you know there are recurring expenses. Make sure you have that list and invest time into understanding how you are going to maintain your future property to protect your investment.

> **Mike, ~23 years old, Director, Solar Energy Professional (owner, rental - single-family property)**

Mike's costs went up quickly due to a rising housing market. Meaning, that because his home increased in value (most likely due to its prime location), he now pays a significant amount more towards taxes on his monthly statement. Depending on how fast the neighborhood changes and the state of the economy, so will change what you pay towards the property. In Mike's case, the property is an investment and not his main residence. Therefore, he can pass the tax bill costs on to his renters.

> **Tash, ~34 years old, entrepreneur (owner, single-family home residence)**

Tash bought her home during the beginning months of the Covid-19 pandemic in 2020. While she did not have all the experience in the world, she did know what to look for. Her directive was to ensure the home was not in the floodplain so that her lender wouldn't require her to purchase and maintain flood insurance. Seek a new build with a great warranty package. She also wanted to live in a gated community for an added measure of safety and security. Lastly, she wanted to be as close as possible to an already established neighborhood with a top ranking for places to live. Deep down inside, she hoped her location would be annexed by the posh neighborhood across the street. With the interest rates plummeting below 3% and the government practically begging consumers to buy and borrow, what she missed was that she could have asked for a better rate package. If she had known that a 2-1 buydown was a financing option, she could have saved even more in her first two years of homeownership while maintaining the excellent rate she already had. Saving on that monthly could have helped pay for the washer, dryer, and refrigerator the developer declined to provide as a value-added incentive to purchase and would have eased a monthly payment. The best option in that case was to ask the lender or seller to contribute towards a buy-down as there can be significant closing costs associated with that strategy and you will want financial support. Especially if it is already an option that just was not presented. As you can tell, each experience is unique. So, now that you have acquired this book and gained insights from fellow first-time homebuyers, you might be wondering how to determine whether you meet the criteria to be considered a first-time homebuyer. If this question is top of mind, here is what qualifies you.

- You have not owned a primary residence during the last three (3) years. – mobile homes that are not affixed to a property do not count.
- The last home you owned was a home with your spouse – you are now divorced or somehow displaced.
- You have a steady income.
- You have at least two (2) years of job history.
- Your credit history is clean.
- Minimum of ~620 credit score – in some cases lower credit scores can qualify but typically come with unfavorable rates.

For complete details, it is advisable to contact your preferred lender. Individual lending programs come with varied requirements. These constitute several key qualities that qualify you as a first-time homebuyer. Nonetheless, the information provided here holds value and can notably influence your homebuying journey, regardless of whether you qualify as a first-time buyer.

In the upcoming chapter, you will hear more about my experiences. Following that, I will lay out how to eat this elephant alongside your team. Before we get into the nitty-gritty of how a transaction is processed, let's walk through who is responsible for what through agency and the parties of agency.

Chapter 2

AGENCY & THE NAR SETTLEMENT

Having proper representation through agency is crucial. It is advisable to seek out the best agent you can find, someone you will genuinely enjoy collaborating with. Believe me, this journey can be quite a rollercoaster. Sometimes it's straightforward but often it's not due to many parties having to come together for consensus. Consensus is what blockchain technology solves for but until technology catches up in this industry, things will continue to be as they are, and the speed of transactions will continue to lag due to the lack of integration of processes and difficulties in succinctly and openly establishing consensus among the parties of the transaction. In summary, the industry lacks the transparency that other industries are moving towards. It stifles buyers and agents alike, hence why I wrote this book.

Speaking of changes and consensus, here is my take on the National Association of Realtors (NAR) settlement that aims to pave a new path for agents, buyers, and sellers. I'm going to briefly describe this from the buyer and owner/seller perspectives. On March 15th, 2024 - NAR reached an agreement with plaintiffs of a lawsuit related to agent commissions and real estate transactions. According to the NAR site, the changes went into effect in August of 2024.

Buyer: Buyers in Texas are no strangers to written representation agreements. Selling agents (buyer reps) moving forward now by law must secure a signed agreement with buyers before showing any property, a standard procedure. However, other states may not yet be acquainted. It is crucial for buyers to actively seek representation and be prepared to review and sign these agreements. Due to the lawsuit, the agent cannot show homes without it. Agents deserve fair compensation and to be under contract for their diligent work, especially now that sellers may not automatically cover the selling agent's commission. While MLS will no longer list commission rates, rates will be listed elsewhere.

It is all about ensuring buyers know exactly what they are getting and what it costs. So, if an agreement is not presented to you as a buyer, ask! This does not seem to apply to showing up at an open house and speaking to an agent but does apply to in-person and live virtual home tours.

Seller: Not much has changed from this perspective. Agent fees have always been negotiable. However, there was a standard of 6% of the sales price which the listing agent would then share with the selling agent. The 6% standard may not go away. That percentage split that goes to the selling agent will likely not be publicizable by law on the MLS but can be posted by the listing agent (who represents the seller) on a third-party site.

Why is having representation so important as a buyer? The homebuying process is not only lengthy but also intricate. The listing agent primarily looks out for the interests of their main client, the seller. Wouldn't you prefer that someone is firmly in your corner? In the upcoming chapter, you'll discover a list of what licensed realtors (also known as real estate agents) do. In brief, they are your guides to discovering your dream home and assessing a property based on your specific needs, budget, and preferred location.

They are not only about finding the right home. They provide you with valuable comparable market data that empowers you to make informed decisions when offering a purchase price and negotiating terms. Sellers benefit similarly; realtors help them determine the likely selling price to avoid prolonged listings that accrue costs, whether it's taxes on a paid-off home or monthly mortgage principal payments (mortgage payments – your note on the home (principal), interest, taxes, and insurance (PITI) on an ongoing one. A skilled agent's insights can potentially save you thousands. Monthly budgets are more accurate. So, look at your PITI and really try and understand if it is something you should move forward with.

Further to the benefits of agency, you might require a contingency in your contract or come across disclosures that are pivotal for your contentment in the home or the health of your investment. Details like Municipal Utilities District (MUD) taxes and homes located in floodplains are essential. Good agents help you avoid unexpected expenses and ensure you're fully informed about your future investment. Agents are your initial set of eyes and indispensable partners, assisting you in navigating confusing terms and identifying potential issues. After all, no one wants to end up with a "lemon" home, better known as a money pit. The distinction between a fixer-upper, a flipper, and a poor investment can be subtle, and your agent can help you differentiate. If they are helping you diligently, they may suggest you use Homes.com for your search. The platform provides overlays such as crime scores, flood maps, and average household income. Homes.com also provides professional videos of neighborhoods that include what the homes look like, where you may want to go to date night, and what schools your kids will attend should you move there. All of which can help you make an informed decision on where you do or do not want to live. Due to the especially important Fair Housing

Act (Anti-Steering), your agent may not be able to provide the details you can find on your own.

Can you buy a home without an agent? Absolutely! However, agents usually have resources inaccessible to the public. One of the benefits is that they often know about opportunities before they hit the market (off-market opportunities). That can help a buyer eliminate competition. They can uncover builder concessions that the other side might not disclose initially. These concessions can significantly enhance the deal for a buyer. Concessions might include additional appliances beyond the original offer. For instance, instead of just a dishwasher, microwave, and oven/stove, you could get an added dryer, and refrigerator. Cash towards closing costs, covered survey expenses, or even a contribution to a rate buydown can be common in certain conditions but not all. While there might be items more tailored to your situation, these are the most typical.

During periods of high interest rates and a cooling-buying market, builders still have products to sell. They begin to offer items like covering 100% of closing costs, providing security systems, installing sprinkler systems, offering significantly improved rates with their preferred lender, and more. However, what truly matters is relationships. Builders need to sustain their businesses as well, so concessions vary based on their ability to maintain profitability and strengthen the industry further.

One last valuable lender incentive worth mentioning is a free 1-2+ year refinance option. This incentive is typically offered by builders who have an in-house lender. They often buy down interest rates to make homes more affordable for buyers and incentivize them to purchase their homes by offering a phenomenal rate. This approach works especially well during tough economic times. Competition can do wonders.

Purchasing a home is undoubtedly a monumental commitment and investment. You want it done right while focusing on your responsibilities, such as organizing your documents and securing financing. If you are not attentive to this, you could miss out on exceptional opportunities. Therefore, it is wise to explore lenders and approach your agent with a pre-qualification letter in hand even if you get requalified through another lender down the line who offers a better package. Always shop rates and packages.

Now, you might wonder, what exactly should you expect from an agent? It is a fantastic question, as some buyers anticipate agents going above and beyond, though sometimes this might not align with the best interests of both parties, especially if an agreement is not yet in place. Agents are not a part of your lending, escrow, or title team. However, they must collaborate with all. Certain deals can be intricate, and staying organized and following the process might not always be clear-cut. That is precisely what this book aims to clarify, providing you with a roadmap to success.

Lastly, there's often confusion about how agents get paid. Can you believe individuals question whether agents should earn compensation? Unbelievable, right?

The general rule is that the seller typically compensates agents, not the buyer. The specific percentage is outlined initially in your buyer representation agreement and the final percentage is in your sales contract which you see and sign before your agent sends it to the seller.

It is no longer assumed that the seller covers the expense. The takeaway through 2024 is that as a buyer you are getting compensated professional support by an individual or team that has a fiduciary responsibility to act in your best interests. What that percentage is and who pays it will need to be negotiated upfront. With the NAR ruling, a buyer may now be more than ever responsible for paying their agent. Payment could take place at closing and through your lending team baking it into your costs. Everything, however, is negotiable. Negotiate upfront.

With the right agent by your side, armed with the knowledge you will gain here, you will be empowered to make sound decisions and navigate the complex world of real estate with confidence.

THE PARTIES AND PARTIES OF REAL ESTATE AGENCY

As a buyer, you hold a pivotal role in the transaction, with responsibilities that align with the cooperation required from all parties involved to ensure a successful outcome. Your responsibilities primarily center on responsiveness to the parties within your transaction and actively fulfilling the tasks you are required to handle or provide. It is worth noting that agents typically do not initiate contact with the opposing party's client, so if this occurs, it's considered unusual. In such cases, it is crucial to promptly involve your own realtor.

Outlined here are the key responsibilities that fall upon the buyer's shoulders:

- What a buyer SHOULD do:
- Arrive at the home tours on time.
- Maintain good to excellent credit throughout the process.
- Seek lender pre-approval right away.
- Respond within a reasonable period.
- Provide earnest money in a timely manner through the prescribed and official channels.
- Remain honest and loyal to your realtor.
- Meet all contract timelines and milestones.

- Be responsive to the lender and title company getting all needed documents the same day as the request.
- Attend the inspection appointment.
- Arrive early for the closing appointment with a photo ID.
- Arrive at the closing appointment with a cashier's check made out to the correct parties as prescribed by the lender.

Once the transaction is complete, change your state ID or driver's license address and file for a homestead exemption should that apply. The address change will enable you to file for a homestead exemption which reduces your tax liability on the property. If you are not going to live there and have purchased the home for investment purposes, there is no need to take this step.

What a buyer SHOULD NOT do:

- Should not schedule showings, use another agent's services outside of the representation contract, or attend open houses without your realtor present.
- Make any big purchases once you are under contract. If you do so, you may be told to start the lending process from the beginning. It is not a fun or glamorous activity. It may also change your ability to afford the property, and you could default on your

estimated closing costs, closing date, concessions, and interest rate if your rate is already locked in.

Buyer's Agent - often referred to as the "Selling Agent," the buyer's agent carries a multifaceted role. Their responsibility goes beyond the writing and execution of contracts and transactions. In this section, we will explore expectations.

Buyer's agents are the driving force that brings buyers to the negotiation table and effectively "sells" the home to them. Their allegiance lies with the buyer's (your) best interests, regardless of whether you're a first-time homebuyer or a seasoned one. Once a representation agreement is signed by the buyer, your agent takes responsibility for managing transactional matters from your perspective. This means that the agent becomes your advocate and ensures your interests are well-represented throughout the process.

It's important to understand that real estate agents have a fiduciary duty, a legal obligation to act in your utmost best interest. This fiduciary role goes beyond a mere professional relationship; it's a commitment to safeguard your interests as if they were their own. Furthermore, agents are mandated to maintain your information for a significant period after the transaction concludes. So, even if you misplace important documents like your property survey or closing materials down the line, you can always turn to your realtor for guidance on what steps to take next. They're here to assist you beyond just the transaction's conclusion.

Your agent: Find an agent that supports your vision & knows the local market well.

What your agent should be providing you with:

1. Information About Brokerage Services (IABS)
2. Information on lenders who have incentives for first-time homebuyers:

   - There is a range of special incentives available that can make homebuying more affordable for you. Your realtor should be able to direct you to lenders offering the best incentives that match your financing needs. Builders often collaborate with in-house lenders, and your agent can make those introductions too.
   - Did you know that first-time homebuyers often put down just 3.5% with an FHA loan, while conventional loans usually require 3%? This contrasts with the 10-20% down payment typically needed for investors and non-first-time homebuyers. If you are a veteran using a VA loan, your down payment is $0.00.

Downpayment Ex.:

- *Property Value: $300,000.00*
- *Investor or not qualified as a first-time buyer downpayment (20%) =$60,000.00*
- *First-time homebuyer applying for a homestead exemption on a conventional loan (3%) = $9,000.00 - a significant difference!*
- *Veteran using a VA loan = $0.00 – an even bigger difference*

3. Comparative Market Analysis (CMA)

- The CMA is essential to helping a buyer understand what the market value of the property is and, therefore, what is a reasonable offer. The market value (not appraisal value) is based on what else is sold that is directly comparable to the property you want to place a bid on. What is meant by directly comparable typically means the home was sold within the last twelve (12) months, it's in the same or similar nearby neighborhood, and it was on the market for a reasonable number of days. If there are not a lot of comparable homes that were sold recently, your agent will need to get creative. However, the CMA is essential to the process.

4. Any other information/addendums and disclosures from the sales contract that are important to concluding a successful and lawful transaction.

- Common Examples: Addendum for Property Subject to Mandatory Membership in a Property Owner's Association, Third Party Financing Addendum, Addendum for Seller's Disclosure of Information on Lead-based Paint, Addendum for Sale of Other Property by Buyer, Right to Terminate Due to Lender's Appraisal, for your protection get a home inspection, etc.

To put it in perspective – the fiduciary responsibilities of a real estate agent are:

Your agent must act in the best interests of you/the client. That means that they should be up to date on all laws and regulations. If they are not, they should have a good source to help navigate murky waters.

The five duties of an agent are:

1. Care
2. Confidentiality
3. Loyalty
4. Obedience
5. Accounting

Below are examples of a buyer's agent not taking care of their responsibilities.

- Will not produce information about their brokerage services.
- They have not provided you with data such as a comparative market analysis upon request or at all.
- They steer you solely to their own listings.
- They are not submitting reasonably requested offers in a timely manner.
- Do not answer your calls or questions within reason.

The bottom line is that you need to find someone who is knowledgeable, cares, and is ready to act with your guidance and on your behalf. Lastly, be specific about your needs, where you want to be, and how long you want to be there. Your agent will also be able to look for what is in your best interest based on your pre-qualification information. So, as mentioned, make sure to provide that upfront.

What a real estate agent is NOT, is a mortgage agent, escrow agent (title), and or property inspector. For support in those areas, reach out to the appropriate professionals.

Buyer's Agent Responsibilities:

- Remain available to answer any questions you have.

- Carefully guide buyers through the lending process and credit scores.
- Research incentives based on buyers' occupation, military service, or home location.
- Maintain knowledge of the local market activity
- Understand current trends in interest rates and local inventory movement.
- Set up and attend appointments to show properties based on your home goals.
- Help you better understand if the property is a right fit.
- When you have identified your ideal home and want to put an offer in – the agent should no longer show other clients that home.
- Ensure the home seller is receiving/accepting the type of financing the buyer can afford. Not all sellers accept all forms of financing.
- Provide estimates of a home's value based on comparable sales prices and not just the list prices.
- Negotiate to get the best deal possible for the buyer. Note that the seller must agree to and accept the terms of the deal to move forward.
- Draft the terms and complete sales contract and legal real estate agreements.
- Manage buyer expectations and experience appropriately.

- Coordinate the entire process between inspector, lenders, title, and seller.
- Open title by making sure the title company receives the fully executed contract and earnest money in a timely manner.

It has become more common for buyers to submit their earnest money to title via online payment. It is the buyer's responsibility to provide the funds to the title company in a timely manner.

Agents should NEVER co-mingle earnest money funds with their own. It is illegal so watch out for it. Remember the earnest money goes to the title company and is a credit towards your purchase. On the check, you will need to state which property the funds are being submitted to. This helps the title company get your funds to the correct file. Cashier's checks have historically been the norm. Who the check is made out to is typically written into the sales contract or will be provided by title. Each title company has its own set of procedures which they will inform you of.

Agents can help to review each lender's offer and provide advice based on their experiences. However, agents are not your lending team and cannot offer financial advice. More that they will, can and should do are below.

- Attend the inspection and discuss areas of concern.
- Attend the final walkthrough.

- Attend the scheduled closing.
- Share information on tax exemptions and walk buyers through the process of how to file.

Listing Agents

The listing agent is like the go-between for the homeowner (seller), your agent, and the home itself. They are the ones who roll up their sleeves and negotiate the details of the sales contract. First thing is first, they put the house up for grabs on the market. They are the ones with the secret sauce to make it stand out in different markets and economic climates. When I say secret sauce, I mean they prepare a CMA. The listing agent and the homeowner team up to create a special agreement that outlines the terms of agency. Everyone needs to be on the same page. That is achieved through a contract. Once their agreement is executed, the agent gets the green light to rock and roll.

To make sure the home gets sold at the right price and in the right way, the listing agent is like a detective. They dig through data from informed official and unofficial sources to find the perfect price tag. They are motivated to make the seller happy and make the deal work.

Listing agents also get a slice of the commission for their hard work in keeping everything on track and helping the home shine. It is important to remember that every agent needs permission from their client to join the party officially. The listing agent does this by communicating their worth to the homeowner (seller), explaining the game plan, and getting a thumbs-up to get things going. Each month that goes by without a sale significantly hurts the owner's bottom line and parties do not get paid until closing. If you must remember one thing about the listing agent, it is that they work with the seller and your agent to finalize the transaction. When you go to sell your first home, you may want to use the same agent you used to purchase it. So, maintain that relationship. Commissions are always negotiable.

Chapter 3:

A LITTLE STORY ABOUT THE ART OF HOMEBUYING

DID RIGHTS AND COULD HAVE DONE BETTERS

In 2020, I finally took the plunge and bought my own slice of Houston, Texas, in the emerging hotspot known as Greater Heights. I went the DIY route as my own agent, spotting something truly special in the peaceful stretch between I-45 610N, 290, and Beltway 8. This neighborhood holds a strategic location in the city's ever-expanding landscape. I proudly completed my journey from the South Side of the city in August 2020.

As I hunted for the perfect home, I kept my eye out for telling signs like bustling retail spots and appealing amenities. For me, the investment was not just about the type of house, but equally about the location. Trust me, LOCATION is the magic word. The right location can make a world of difference, translating into thousands more in your pocket over the years. Just be cautious, though; take a page from Mike's experience. Even though he made a savvy investment, he ended up with a heavier tax bill. Quick tax tip: if your property is a secret gem that has not hit the market yet, consider asking agents not to list it. Listing a property can tip off the county assessor and lead to a higher tax bill sooner down the line. It is not a deal-breaker to list it, but it is a nifty trick to remember.

Sure, the Greater Heights area is not exactly Bellaire or West U., but it nestles perfectly within a cluster of charming neighborhoods, offering spacious lots and a canopy of mature trees. The agent who won me over was Rachael. She confidently sold me on the idea that the home was a smart, energy-efficient choice and that the neighborhood had a bright future. She even had her finger on the pulse of who else was jumping on board in the community. Rachael knew exactly what buttons to press. This was not just about a house; it was about an investment. The neighborhood was on the cusp of change, and the possibilities were wide open. So, here is where I hit the mark and a few spots, in hindsight, I could have done better.

A Little Story About The Art Of Homebuying | 29

What I did right:

Grabbed a License for Less: Back in 2016, I earned a real estate (RE) license without breaking the bank - see the acknowledgments. That decision saved me around $7,000 to $9,000, on top of helping me negotiate a better price. Getting that license turned out to be like unlocking a treasure trove. Not only did it let me tap into a network of local real estate insights and connections, but it also afforded me information to help me make smarter decisions down the road alongside other agents.

Searched Strategically: I played detective in worthy neighborhoods. I looked at areas that had already blossomed and observed what businesses were popping up. My exposure to commercial retail professionals came in handy because I could read the patterns better. Here is a sneak peek: some businesses love hanging out together. For example, in Houston, you will find Home Depot, Lowes, and Chick-fil-A teaming up in prime spots. PetSmart is never far behind, and Whole Foods and HEB are the rockstars of grocery stores. In 2018, after Hurricane Harvey but before the pandemic, the opening of Whole Foods 365 Market kicked off a wave of gentrification in Greater Heights. Whole Foods brought in a fresh brand tailored to the neighborhood's composite. HEB joined the party in 2019. These retailers are like puzzle masters when it comes to picking their locations—thinking about supply chains, growth potential, and all. Once I had a shortlist, I dug deeper into what I wanted, like a gated community for safety and easy access to outdoor fun. The bottom line? The pros know their game.

Checked In During Tough Times: I got lucky—I was in Houston during Hurricane Harvey. That meant I could check out different neighborhoods and see how they held up. Even if a property looks like a dream and the location is perfect, you have got to think about risks too. In Houston, I went for investments away from flood-prone zones, but close enough to bayous to take advantage of fun city infrastructure. By making a smart call, flood insurance became optional, putting money back in my pocket. Harvey taught us that floods do not play favorites, but smart design can help protect homes. Making the right location choice turned out to be a money-saver. If your home is in or near a flood-prone area and you are financing it, brace yourself for flood insurance. It is an added expense that's often accompanied by a steep deductible. Stay dry and avoid flood hazard areas if your home isn't new and ready to take on the aftermath of heavy storm systems.

Picked the Right-Fit Lender: Who you rely on can make an enormous difference. First-time buyers can get serious assistance. In Houston and for qualified candidates, up to a whopping $30,000 while it lasts. Remember, different cities have different goodies. Lenders even offer discounts if you take a first-time homebuyer course. Sometimes it is a smart choice, other times it is a requirement with a financial perk. If you do go through a government program, it is just as important to understand the terms at which the borrowing comes at a cost of. Some programs only offer partial ownership and require the property to be your primary residence. You may also be required to hold the property for a certain period (months, or years).

Piggy-backed on Developer Research: If a big-shot builder or real estate company is making waves in an up-and-coming area, do not blink and miss it. Check out what they have got all over the city. These folks do their homework just like those retail pros. Get someone impressive like Rachael to break down the pros and cons of your options. Even if you are sure you've got it figured out, you might just discover something new that could totally change your game.

Gave the drainage a thorough check: If you are eyeing a particular home or street, give it a literal rain check. On a rainy day (think cats and dogs), see how well the drainage handles the deluge.

Negotiated some fun concessions: Concessions are items that sweeten the pot for buyers and may help sellers move product (homes) faster. The concessions I received were a significant price decrease around $30k. I approached the developer and asked them to build a bench into the master shower. I wanted it done because I saw it in another one of their homes and liked it. Because I had seen it, I knew they could easily do it. They hooked me up with two master closets instead of one (still the best thing ever!). It came at the cost of a landing. In a three (3) bedroom home on my own, I can land anywhere. My wardrobe, however, cannot. Remember that the seller/builder had to agree to any changes made. Some builders build according to plan and that is it. Your agent can make the ask but the sellers do not have to agree to anything. They especially will not if there is a material cost to change. Below are common enough items you and your agent can look to negotiate as perks.

- The seller agrees to pay for closing costs.
- The seller covers the cost of new appliances.
- The seller covers the cost of fixes and or enhancements.
- The seller pays for the survey or title insurance.
- While title insurance may not be mandatory, it is recommended and, in many cases, if not all, lenders require it. So, expect it to be baked into your closing costs.
- The seller covers the buyer's moving costs.
- The lender agrees to pay for title and/or survey.
- You get the idea. The list goes on. Note that negotiations can result in a win for the buyer, seller, and all parties involved simultaneously.

What I should have also considered

Homeowners Association (HOA): HOA fees can be insane, even a little rude. HOAs are businesses that have costs that rarely go down. Make sure you know what neighborhood policies are, how much the HOA charges, and what goes towards that cost. Speaking of businesses, ensure that your HOAs do not tie your hands by not letting you monetize your property. You may not want to, but it is always nice to have options. Specific examples are long-term & short-term rental options, and what physical improvements are within policy guidelines. On the lines of sustainable living, does your HOA take issue with solar panels? You should find out.

HOA Drama: In a bold move, the HOA tried hiking up our yearly bill by a whopping $500.00 the very next year after I moved in. The community was not complete, and I could not think of a single item that would have increased their bill by $500.00 per owner, per year. I rallied my neighbors, and guess what? One of them was a real estate accountant (lucky break!). We rolled up our sleeves, self-audited the HOA, and uncovered a jaw-dropping $40,000.00 discrepancy in their books. I had a strong inkling this was happening, but without my neighbors and a community-wide threat to officially audit them, they kept denying it. Eventually, the correction was made, but not before we pushed them hard. It also took a minute for them to provide the documentation. They did a victory dance after reluctantly setting things right. Curious why this little scandal happened?

Behind the Scenes: It all boiled down to the developer stumbling in the second year of the Covid-19 pandemic. Lumber theft, supply chain snags, and a shortage of skilled labor threw them off course. Yep, even the big players faced chaos during Covid-19. Here is the kicker—when they tried to up our fees, they still owned the lion's share of the project. That gave them the majority vote in the HOA committee, a club that excluded us common folks. The developer's logic was that since they were grappling with unprecedented challenges, we should all chip in. But we had a different tune and we turned up the volume.

Beware that if short-term leases are permissible, your neighbors can also partake. Rowdy crowds may show up for parties and all sorts of inconveniences may occur. In one case I witnessed, an Airbnb guest had a party around the corner from my home. Their guest's cars ended up blocking the garage of almost every resident in the community. Can you imagine not being able to leave your house because someone you do not even know and can't find is parked directly in front of your garage? Yeah. They were loud, left a stream of trash in the community, and then proceeded to get on a bullhorn in front of the house and chat with all the residents after the police officers left for probably the second time that night. No, they did not shut the party down, in fact, more people poured in. They did promise to turn the music down. The bullhorn was the final act of the night.

From that incident, we also learned how powerless we were. The community wrote the HOA and demanded a contract with a towing company and signs that confirmed the rules of engagement for visitor parking. It may take a while to get done, but it is worth the fight. Trial by fire has been the savage reality of our experience. Note that it is not your real estate agent's responsibility to manage your community or insensitive neighbors after closing.

Easements: There was an easement on my property. I was not informed that it could not be moved. I should have asked. It is something I always check for now. The fiber optics stations were not installed in a straight line. One of them ended up in my backyard and to get to it, the service provider must enter my property. They can enter and dig up my garden to bury lines for other homes. Unfortunately, I picked that lot for a more compelling reason. I honestly thought it could be a quick removal of the box. It was more complicated than that. The bottom line is that it is not going away. I will add that it has been a hassle especially when I want to get some sun and the fiber optics guy gets to join. However, the community is now complete, and the worst may have passed. Find a developer that designs their communities with these petty inconveniences in mind.

On another note, if you are looking for new construction make sure the builder has the correct infrastructure in place. There were 1-2 gated communities in my area that did not have internet service due to no fiberoptic infrastructure. I felt for them. Their battle went on for months during the worst months of Covid. The easement item was not ideal but at least I had infrastructure for the internet.

Le train: The first morning I woke up in my new space, I experienced the train. It was way down the road but clear. The area was not yet made into a quiet zone. It still is not. When I inquired with a community leader, I was given a comprehensive list of other priority items the original community had. Some of those items were gentrification, extreme poverty, and rising property values that is increasing taxes. The results were that long-time locals could no longer afford their properties and were being forced to leave their neighborhoods. It was heartbreaking to think I was a part of this. There had also been a concern about how developers were going about building the infrastructure for the new communities and how that could affect overall flooding in properties right next door. The thunderous train was at the bottom of that list, as it should have been. After years, do I still hear it? Yes, but it is not all that bad. Still, I should have known the sound may carry or at least asked around about if it was a quiet zone having seen the tracks. Did I mention the roosters at dawn?

Snowvid: The major Texas freeze week of 02.15.2021 was a trip. It left the city bruised but not broken. Before the water to the city shut off for days, my aunt Sabrina gave me learned advice to fill my bathtub with water. We usually drink filtered water rather than bottled water. So, we would have been dehydrated as the stores were out of everything. Let us not forget that we needed to cook clean and use the restrooms! I made the executive decision and filled the tub prior to the water going off. We had another form of water supply after we pooled resources with other refugees. In my second bathroom, I settled for just a shower. Perhaps having another tub would have been wise. I made sure to get a bucket. On a positive note, I also got to experience energy efficiency at its best. The home remained appropriately insulated throughout. My energy bill was more than reasonable. Lastly, with a stroke of luck 2 days in, I noticed that the porta potties from the construction team were still there. Not everyone was so lucky. Consider how you might store water in case of an emergency.

Solar: I assumed the HOA would not oppose solar panels on our homes. However, it is always a good idea to check with your future HOA. If you can get your hands on their policies for review, even better. You do not want to move into a community where you cannot make the improvements you desire. Especially if they advantage you financially or increase the value of your home. Not all communities have HOAs. You will be informed if yours does during the purchasing process.

Along the lines of energy and solar, a consideration for a backup power supply after your purchase may be to invest in a battery. Immediately you might think of a generator. However, after experiencing the intense storms that have come through the Gulf Coast cities, I can tell you that some generators require you to use gas – which may not be accessible during an emergency. Because generators are typically fueled by gas, owners need to leave their garage open and perhaps have the generator stored outside. This leaves your home and generator vulnerable to theft. In general, I have long thought about solar and consulted with Mike Phung, who was mentioned earlier in the reading about what that investment looks like. The main question is, do you have an HOA, and if you do, will they allow solar panels to be installed on your property?

Private Mortgage Insurance (PMI): Being a first-time homebuyer and being prescribed PMI on a conventional loan allowed me to put only 3% into the initial down payment and keep more capital on hand. I read the terms of the agreement that in two (2) years on the dot, I would be eligible for removal given that certain criteria were met. The stars aligned and I applied. Because of inconsistent industry standards, I had to do so twice. The mortgage company and appraisers dragged it out for months. That cost me approximately $1,000.00 throughout that period still paying a PMI note that didn't need to exist. The first appraisal/opinion of value was off by $30,000.00 - disaster. I contested and it was a full-on battle. The second time,

I took into consideration the state of the industry and removed any pictures of myself, my family, and any art that may trigger bias in the appraiser. My friend Liz, provided photos of her beautiful family who are of European descent. My neighbor, Jose, showed my home so the appraiser had no clue what I looked like. That did the trick. I was then able to prove that I had enough equity in the property to save over$2,400/year over the next few years. If I had to go back, I would have tried to find a way out of it all together.

Also, yes, in this industry, it matters very much what you look like and who you are. The first appraiser went as far as to check my LinkedIn profile to get a gander at what I did for a living, and he had the advantage of having met me in person. We had a pleasant encounter at my home. I read both reports thoroughly. They were completed around two (2) months apart and the market had cooled off since the first one was done. The comps were night and day. An appraiser can easily devalue your home should they feel like it or believe that you do not fit the bill for honest treatment. Appraisers in this instance are contracted by mortgage companies. Fiscally, it is not in the collector's best interest to remove your PMI obligation. So, they tend to not crack down on potential dishonesty and provide plenty of room for subjectivity. I think you get the picture. Oops!

Chapter 4:

HOW TO EAT THIS ELEPHANT

HOME SHOPPING

While many buyers are enthusiastic about exploring all their options, real estate agents will encourage you to narrow down your choices to homes that truly align with your needs. This approach is wise. It's important to get pre-qualified at the earliest opportunity, so you have a clear numerical understanding of what alignment means. Moreover, if you are aware of your monthly housing budget, try to determine the price range that fits comfortably within it. This monthly strategy offers the most realistic approach to financial accuracy.

Your credit score significantly impacts the interest rates you will be eligible for, thus affecting your home affordability. A higher credit score provides advantages. A credit score of 640 and above is considered reasonable. Before seeking pre-qualification, it is advisable to check your credit score using your bank's mobile app. Furthermore, maintaining or improving your score throughout the homebuying process is crucial. The advice consistently ties back to the recommendation to avoid major financial changes during this period. The more credit you use, the worse it is for your score. It also affects your debt-to-income ratio which helps lenders determine how much home you can afford. I advise speaking with a credit professional if your score is questionable. Paying off the RIGHT debt to afford more is essential. A credit professional can help you determine what to pay off first and what will have the most significant impact on your score. In many cases, lenders can provide you with immeasurable feedback on credit score repair and usage. In either case, consult a professional.

Open Houses:

Open houses are a fun way to both see a home and learn more about a neighborhood from a realtor who may or may not be the selling agent. That is right. The agent you meet at the open house event may be looking for buyers to connect with and shop homes with. If you pop in but you are working with an agent, politely let them know but still ask general questions about the home. **Take note that due**

to the NAR settlement, selling agents are now required to have an agreement signed by you the buyer before showing a home – I doubt this applies to an open house but get ready for it. If there were questions that could not be answered through the agent at the open house, let your agent know to reach out to the listing agent for more information.

Home Tours:

Are the actual number of rooms and bathrooms that were listed consistent with what you see on the property? That's right. Not all is what it seems until you get there. Boots on the ground is the only way to properly evaluate a home. But that is nothing new. Touring a property is real estate 101. If you are far away, get someone to conduct a video tour while you work on getting to the physical property.

I have toured a lot of homes. It is easy to get swept up in the newness of the space and the fun features like soft closing drawers and a gorgeous gas range. While we as realtors will indulge with you, our main goal is to see if there are any major issues or items to investigate.

Many homes look nothing like the photos presented online. Some homes look better and some look far worse. Seeing a home in person is essential to the process. I have on more than one occasion arrived at a home to check it out and said aloud, "Is this the right property?" on more than one occasion. If you are out of state, arrange for a video tour through your local realtor. Some listing agents provide 3D tours which are super helpful.

What is possible to see on the roof? Some faults are easily spotted from the ground. A heavy tree trunk on top of a roof is hard to miss. Although they tend to increase the property value, trees that are too close take-out roofs and foundations. Does the floor feel uneven? If anything seems off, you could be looking at undisclosed or disclosed foundation problems which are typically costly. If you still like the home, you can get a cost estimate from a professional foundation repair firm which the seller may already have on hand, and ask for the money in concessions from the seller. If there is a great big tree close to the house, you could be looking at foundation issues from the point of purchase and in the future. My favorite homes are the older ones that have gone ahead and fixed the foundation, updated the roof, and replaced an old HVAC system.

HVAC systems are also important. If you see a system on the property, you may be able to get warranty information and or at the very least details that will help you understand the age of the unit. Age matters in efficiency. Efficiency affects your bill. Not all listing agents are made the same and they may not have that information on hand -electricity bills and/or age. In that case, it is up to you and your agent to gather what you can. Systems that are up in age can also be costly to repair or replace.

Mold? Do you smell it at the home? If so, speak with your agent about the seller's willingness to get the home remediated. The inspection will reveal what you may or may not suspect. That is why inspections are crucial. Yes, even with new construction.

What does visitor parking look like and what might your future neighbors be like? Do you have fencing, or might you need to bake fencing into the equation?

Most if not all modern homes are built with energy-efficient materials that can help keep those electricity bills in check. This typically applies to windows while air conditioning control units may be programable smart devices. Open floorplans have become popular in Texas and fun but subtle lighting like under mounts in the kitchen over the counters and under the cabinets has always been my favorite touch by builders. It highlights and enhances beautiful countertops. If they are LED lights, they may even help with the energy bill while making for great ambiance. Remember that older homes with taller ceilings are gorgeous but may produce a higher energy bill if the home is not efficient.

Trim and wall molding done tastefully can make all the difference in resale and new construction. Think about that should you want to approach your builder to produce a slightly elevated interior finish within reason by having a fancier trim to frame your walls and molding that is in good condition. For a foundation, you may want to pick the foundation that works best for the soil in your search area. Builders in that area will have expertise on what works best. If it is a resale you can inquire about foundation issues which will also be revealed in your inspection. Various soils carry certain foundations either better worse or equally. That is especially if you are looking in areas with high flood potential or a coastal property. You can typically look at the home and determine which is which type of foundation. In either case, you want to make sure the soil is sloping away from your home to prevent sitting water near your foundation. Your inspector should walk you through each aspect of the physical property, including the foundation and sloping.

One last thought about home tours and the search is that there seem to be supply deficiencies in homes with both ground floor and upstairs living spaces. Think about the privacy that layout provides should you have guests, in-laws visiting, or want to monetize one of the rooms. Because it seems to be a rarity, it could be an added advantage when you sell.

Chapter 5:

HOW TO EAT THIS ELEPHANT

THE PURCHASING PROCESS

The question for every aspiring new homeowner should be, how am I/are we going to eat this elephant? It is a brave question that deserves strategic action.

You will need a good real estate agent and lending team if you are not paying cash in full and aren't an agent yourself. If It is a new developer or builder, you want to know that they are competent. That means that you entrust that they have done the proper environmental and sustainable building due diligence. If a developer is properly invested and committed, everyone wins. Next, we are going to take a dive into some of the most important steps. The goal here is to give you a better understanding of the order of operations and relieve some of the overwhelming anxiety as you will know why things should and need to occur in this way.

Pre-Qualification (This is the first thread that leads to the underwriting process):

1. Having this step complete will signal to your real estate agent that you are a serious buyer. A real commitment takes place. Once an agent is committed to you and you know who and what their brokerage stands for, your homebuying success is their fiduciary responsibility. To commemorate this, agents will present you with an Information About Brokerage Services (IABS) form and a buyer representation agreement. Once signed, your journey commences. Note: It is required by law to have a buyer review and sign the IABS form. While it is not a requirement (yet) by law to have the representation agreement signed, you will find that it becomes an essential piece of the transaction on the brokerage side and should be executed.

2. Many buyers look at homes and determine where they want to be prior to the previous step. However, the very start of this process has much to do with what you can purchase and that may end up informing on where or what you can purchase in each market. You know how it is, you build the romance up over

a few sexy home propositions and then reality steals your thunder.

3. Through the pre-qualification process you will find out that you can either afford more, less, or equal to the amount of home you have been seeking. Pre-qualification also helps your agent provide you with the most relevant opportunities. If you are like I am/was, I was doing drive-throughs of where I wanted to live, and it turned out that I wasn't too far off the mark of what I could afford. How could you not get out there and take a look if you are in the same city? The information is right at your fingertips through the latest applications.

4. That's why this step is so important. You want to shop with purpose and be informed so that you are connecting with the best opportunities in your playing field. Perhaps this is the part where you find out if you need a bit of financial support or if you can purchase something on your own vs needing gift funds or a raise at work. Pre-qual is typically quick and is most commonly done via a lender form online.

5. Typical mortgage pre-qualification requirements by a lender are but are not limited to:

    i. All income sources.

    ii. Employment Information (verification)

    iii. Pay Stubs - 30-60 days.

iv. Tax Returns

v. W2s

vi. Bank Statements (2-3 months)

Deal Processing – Securing Financing (Loan Application): After getting pre-qualified, you are going to shop around with your agent.

1. The next steps are to finalize your property choice by presenting your offer and winning the bid. Your financing information goes into the contract that your realtor will write and may pass through their broker for a second set of eyes. They next get your signature before delivering the contract to the listing agent that represents the seller. Smart agents speak to the listing agent before submittal to better understand the condition of the seller and the sentiment of the listing agent. That is to say, you should know if the offer is close to or is acceptable to the seller. Try and work smart as contracts can take a lot of time to put together, especially when there are addendums and disclosures to dig up. You will need to read and review every single document. The disclosures are important. If you are making an all-cash offer, the above still applies with the added benefit that the transaction process is typically much faster. It is faster due to not having to process the loan otherwise known as underwriting.

2. If all terms are agreed upon, next you will go under contract with the negotiated and agreed upon terms. You are officially under contract when all parties have signed the contract. You now need to deliver the earnest money (do not forget your receipt as you will need a record of it). Remember, earnest monies go towards the downpayment or other closing costs. You do get credit for it. It is not an extra charge. The earnest money payment lets the seller know you truly intend to purchase. It is skin in the game prior to closing.

3. After all the previously mentioned is complete, you still need your loan processed. The underwriting process for your mortgage does not happen until the appropriate amount of information is gathered and submitted to underwriting. In some cases, lenders will ask you to resubmit documents to apply for the mortgage. At some point you will want to lock in your interest rate, which is what it costs or the price to borrow money– the rate at which you will borrow money. This can happen right after the fully executed contract is delivered to your loan officer, which should be right after everyone signs. Your lender will guide you regarding when the best time is to lock in the rate. The whole process can take 30-45 + days if financed. Cash deals close much sooner as underwriting does not take place. Your realtor accounts for the time it will likely take to close by placing an estimated close date within the contract. So, feel free to check back in on what

your executed contract says and plan accordingly. If you miss your closing date, fines and fees are most likely associated after a certain period past the agreed upon date. In short, you want to close on time and if you have an option period in your contract, make sure your due diligence is completed prior to the number of days your option period states. What is an option period? It is a specific number of days that you can legally get out of your executed contract and have your escrow funds returned penalty-free. Use it wisely.

4. In addition to the contract, you will get an initial loan estimate from your lender. The loan officer will also provide you with the cost of the loan. Information and estimates about the loan are known as the initial disclosers.

You will want to work with a firm who has an electronic setup. There will be plenty of communication around documents to review and signatures needed, so, buckle up.

Expect these items to be a part of the process:

1. **Home Appraisal** – Because what homes are sold for and how much they are appraised for does not always match up. If those two things do not align, you may not get the loan amount you anticipated from the bank or mortgage company. More importantly, the bank uses this number to help confirm the value. If a lien is placed on your property, the banks are typically

in a prime position to take it back and they want to know exactly what the asset is worth at the point of sale as they may one day have it on their books as an asset or liability if it's under water. An underwater asset is where what is owed exceeds what it is worth. Lenders also want to ensure that the loan size is appropriate. Hence the appraisal of value.

2. **Survey** – Always get a survey. Think about it, how else would you prove where your property line begins and ends during a dispute? Yes, disputes happen. Title companies also require it. There may already be a survey that is acceptable to title but it's good to go through title should you need to purchase one so that you know it is title company approved and by their standards defensible in court. The cost of surveys typically ranges from $400-$1,000.

3. **Title Work** – The history of the property'title will be confirmed. If there is not a clear title, ownership may be in jeopardy should another party claim title somewhere down the line. What is the title exactly?It helps determine ownership and so the current owner transfers that ownership interest to you at the point of sale. If there is an issue with title and other claims on the property, the title company will defend your right to ownership in court. That is what title insurance is for.

4. **Shop Home Insurance:** Shopping for home insurance is a critical step in the home-buying process, as it

provides essential benefits for both homeowners and lenders. Lenders typically mandate home insurance, making it an essential part of your requirements. While you might not have the freedom to shop around for all aspects of your closing, you have the flexibility to shop for home insurance. The required coverage is often determined by your lender, and it is your responsibility to compare rates to meet this requirement. Keep in mind that home insurance is a mandatory condition of your loan. To gain clarity on what aspects you can shop rates for and what you cannot, it is advisable to consult your lender. The importance of purchasing home insurance cannot be overstated. If you are unsure about the process, don't hesitate to seek guidance from your agent or lender for referrals and advice. An old friend of mine, John Bramblett, currently works as the Director of Strategic Initiatives & Partner Relations for Stewart Insurance. He was adamant that I expand this section. As usual, he was right, insurance is huge and is typically mandatory through your lender.

Top reasons to purchase home insurance:

1. Mortgage Requirement: Meets lender conditions for mortgage holders.
2. Property Protection: Coverage against damage from various perils, including fire, theft, and wind.

3. Belongings Coverage: Replacement or repair of belongings like furniture and electronics.
4. Liability Protection: Financial safeguard if someone is injured on your property.
5. Living Expenses: Coverage for temporary housing during repairs.
6. Peace of Mind: Security and confidence in unforeseen situations.
7. Legal Support: Covers legal costs in case of lawsuits.
8. Financial Security: Prevents major setbacks by aiding rebuilding efforts. Understanding your policy's details is crucial for optimal protection.

For your protection get an inspection:

- Inspectors are an important partner in this process. You could lose out on something an inspector missed. It is an inspector's job to tell you the physical condition of a property.
- The inspector I hired missed something that I had to point out around 2-3 times on different occasions. The builder had missed cutting through a window in the master bathroom. The developer denied it up until the day of closing where I was able to physically point it out again during the new construction final walkthrough session where I would need to sign off on my satisfaction with the condition of the home.

The window appeared on the outside of the home, but not the inside. I let the inspector know as he had not even noticed. He sent a mundane text back about adding it as an item in his inspector's report. It made me wonder what other details he missed. The feeling stuck so much that before my one (1) year builder's warranty was up, I paid for a seasoned professional to do another full inspection so it would be clear what needed more work by the builder and in what priority to fight for items on the punch list. It is a rare thing to win the whole battle. If I had gone with the better inspection service the first time, I could have saved around $600 and perhaps gotten the developer to do more work that was supposed to be done upfront. Your inspection plays a key role in the purchasing process and in your overall experience.

- Who you choose to inspect your home does count. It is just a fact of life and it's better to know upfront from trained professionals who stand by their work what may need some capital expenditure and which party may be responsible. Ask your realtor if they know of any excellent inspectors to work with. Get a recommendation list for prime inspectors from your agent. They know who is going to do an excellent job.

Underwriting:

AVOID these red flags that underwriters look for:

1. No monthly income
2. Job change (company hopping)
3. Outstanding taxes
4. DO NOT make any large purchases and do not make any large money moves during this process.
5. Try not to get a divorce or change your marital status!

Stay close to your loan processor. Their part is critical to getting you to and through underwriting. It is a tough and laborious process so get your calming beads out and stick with the process. Part of the process is avoiding the red flags mentioned previously.

The underwriter's role is to verify the documents you submit meet their requirements. They ensure that there is minimal risk in providing you with a loan. Buyers with better credit tend to get offered better terms and a preferred interest rate. There are different types of loans. During your search, your agent can tell you which sellers are willing to take the following type of financing that you may be eligible for: Conventional, FHA, VA, cash offer.

Once the underwriter completes their process, you are qualified for the loan and receive it, or you do not, and you can reapply. The conditions under which you are approved will be presented. To be clear, there are certain conditions that must be met. Then and only then will you get the "Clear to Close" as a final step in the approval process.

Some hang-ups may be that they want you to submit/resubmit items such as but not limited to: letters of clarification, current bank statements, current pay stubs, etc. Resubmission will be executed through your loan processor who will then re-submit the items to the underwriter. This part of the process is often stressful and can be lengthy in some cases. That is why it is important to connect with a lender that has seasoned loan officers and top-tier underwriters. Let us not forget that poor lending practices were the leading cause of the Great Recession that spanned from ~2007-2009. So, expect some level of scrutiny born from what was learned.

Once you have a fully executed contract and all disclosures signed by the seller and all parties involved, and you have a clear to close from your lender you are now waiting to close. The estimated closing date is provided in the sales contract

Remember: Have your inspection done well before closing and provide plenty of time for the sellers to take care of any loose ends such as room conversions or a paint job and other items outlined by your inspector. You could even say it is best practice to have this done right after your contract is executed. It will also depend on how ready the home is.

Preparation for Closing:

You are almost there. So, give yourself a big pat on the back because that is freaking amazing. Yes, you! At this time, you can plan your move and prepare your pets for the journey to your new space.

a. Your next gift is a Closing Disclosure (CD). The CD is a statement of what funds you will bring to closing. It is a requirement by law that lenders provide this to you at least three (3) days before closing. Yes, your closing costs are just as important as everything else. Within the CD you will have the final terms of the loan and more details about the transaction. The information on the CD should closely resemble the estimates you would have received at the start of this process from your lender. Make sure that fees have not skyrocketed and there are no extras on your tab. Your real estate agent is not your lender but can help you review the initial estimate alongside the closing disclosure. So, make sure they have a copy on hand. You will most likely need a second set of eyes. Review the CD well before closing so that lenders will have an opportunity to make necessary revisions to the document and not delay closing.

b. On closing day, you will need:

c. The amount listed in the CD to close (of certified funds – cashier's check)

d. An acceptable form of photo identification

e. Finally

f. The closing documents are signed by both sides of the deal on typically the day of closing.

g. That is all she wrote! You will be presented with your documents and the keys either at or after closing. Some sellers leave them with the title company for transfer at closing and sometimes other arrangements are made. I recommend you get them at closing. Your deed, which is the document you get stating you own the home, is validated by title and given to you. If you would like an additional copy down the line, you can request one via your County Recorder's office. Marriage Note: Regardless of if this is a joint purchase, in the state of Texas, no matter who is on the deed, the property is owned equally by both parties.

Chapter 6:

BE A SAVVY BUYER

SUGGESTIONS FOR WHAT TO LOOK FOR IN A COMMUNITY

There are a lot of criteria that you can look at when finding the right-fit community. This aims to give you a head start so that you can be a savvy buyer.

1. Community Planning Initiatives
2. Concept (open vs closed)
3. Crime & Safety
4. Fencing
5. Garage apartment
6. Garage Space

7. In a brand-new subdivision – make sure infrastructure and services are available for high-speed internet and connectivity. When I first moved into my home, I double-checked as a community down the road didn't have infrastructure. They all moved in and discovered that they couldn't work from home during the start of the pandemic…for months.
8. Layout
9. Major retailers – especially for groceries
10. Median rent (in case you want to explore the property as an investment or have a garage apartment that you want to rent out for extra income.
11. Nearby amenities
12. Nearby services
13. Nightlife
14. Pool access or the possibility of installing one (1)
15. Proximity to Parks & Recreation
16. Public Transportation
17. Railway proximity
18. Reviews
19. Safety
20. School Districts/Zoning (not all cities have zoning)
21. Single Standing vs Connected Homes (townhomes)
22. Square Footage

23. Storage Space
24. These are other key considerations for the space need: Two (2) floors vs one (1) Upstairs vs downstairs living, visitor parking accommodations, and yard space.

CONCLUSION

Here are your immediate next steps after purchasing a primary residence. They are important and by reading this thoroughly, you will save time and energy in a space that can be confusing.

File for your homestead exemption.

Why file for a homestead exemption? Based on what you qualify for it can significantly reduce the tax burden on your home. Think of it as a discount on your tax bill due to the home being your primary residence. Specifically, the exemption takes your home's value as determined by the appraisal district you purchased in and removes part of the value from taxation. You will not pay taxes on the full amount of the appraised value of your home. Investment homes pay the full tax amount unless owners submit the necessary deductions. Not all deductions qualify. Check with your tax expert for more on what does and does not qualify. So, yes! Claim your Homestead Exemption if it applies to your situation! Up next are details on how to do that.

Change your address on your driver's license ID.

The process cannot begin until you complete this step! Your change of address can easily be accomplished online through your DMV's website. If not, visit your local DMV office to complete this step.

Resale vs new construction homes

Newly built homes are straightforward because they have not been lived in and you will be the first to apply for the homestead exemption.

If another homestead exemption on the property has been filed for that year, your exemption will start the following year. You can wait to file; however, I recommend you file as soon as possible in both cases. The application will be rolled over appropriately, and you will have taken care of a big-ticket item. The case of another exemption typically happens on a resale home where the previous owner has the exemption.

Check your local appraisal district's website (Houston > HCAD.org). Search for your address and check to see if your name appears as the property owner.

This can be taken care of through title at closing and typically populates within a few weeks after the closing date. However, in the instance that it is not taken care of at closing, it is up to you as the homeowner to request a change of ownership. There should be a form on the very same site to do so electronically. The title of the form you are looking for should be something like: "Request to Correct Name or Address on Real Property Account."

Finally, check out those appliances and home goods sales! When you close matters. I specifically chose August for my home's closing. The holiday sales that occur in the third and fourth quarters of the year are awesome.

Congratulations! Given the information provided in the previous chapters, you should now have a solid understanding of the steps involved in buying your first home. Go ahead and read this more than once as there is a lot of information. That information includes how best to determine your budget, home shopping, underwriting, and closing the deal. Remember, finding your property starts with knowing what your budget is. Think seriously about what you can actually afford each month. The loan prequalification process is a start or producing a proof of funds letter if you are a cash buyer. Find the right agent and you all can achieve anything. The fact that you are reading this book implies that you have taken big strides toward realizing your dream of homeownership and finding the best team to close on your dream property.

As you navigate this exciting journey, remember to stay focused on your goals and trust your instincts. Don't be afraid to ask lots of questions and lean on experts when and where needed. Take time to ask the tough questions, and find a property that fits, both now and in the future.

Feel free to reach out with more ideas for what else the real estate community could do better in advising buyers on prior to a first-time home purchase. Make sure it falls within the real estate expertise and would add value to the experience. Remember, your real estate agent is not your lending, title, and or insurance agent. But they can help you navigate the process and get you the best purchase terms that the seller is willing to accept. Read and reference this as many times as needed throughout your homebuying experience. We as an industry understand just how complex this can be and openly welcome the challenge. Finally, thank you for joining me. I wish you all the best as you embark on this new chapter in your life.

Happy house hunting!"

Made in the USA
Middletown, DE
12 October 2024